101 Tips for Becoming a $100,000-a-Year Freelance Writer

Dawn Josephson

Copyright © 2014 Dawn Josephson

ISBN: 0-9744966-3-4
ISBN-13: 978-0-9744966-3-4

For more information on Dawn Josephson's consulting, coaching, or other services or products, please use the contact information that suits you best:

Dawn Josephson
The Master Writing Coach™

Phone: (904) 685-8064
Email: dawn@masterwritingcoach.com
Web: www.masterwritingcoach.com

DEDICATION

To freelance writers everywhere.
Never give up on your dreams.

CONTENTS

Acknowledgments   i

Introduction   1

1   Setting Up Shop   2

2   Marketing Your Writing Business   5

3   Day-to-Day Success   9

4   Working with Clients Effectively   15

5   Sustained Business and Personal Growth   19

About the Author   23

ACKNOWLEDGMENTS

To my family, thank you for seeing me through yet another project.

To my husband, David Josephson, thank you for your willingness to participate in this project and for your unwavering love and support.

Finally, to all my friends, both old and new, thank you for your support, your kindness, and your unending desire to improve your craft. You are what make the writing process so rewarding.

INTRODUCTION

Have you ever dreamed of working from home as a full-time freelance writer? You're not alone. Every year thousands of people make the leap to start their own freelance business. Unfortunately, many do not succeed. Why? It's not because they aren't skilled writers; rather, they lack the know-how needed to succeed as a freelancer.

This booklet gives you the insider secrets you need to successfully start, market, run, and sustain a profitable freelance business. In fact, by using the information in these pages, you can quickly and easily become a six-figure a year freelance writer, all while working from the comfort of your home. Yes, it will take some work on your part. But the rewards are worth it!

Setting Up Shop

1. **Schedule time for writing.** You can easily get sidetracked with household chores, life's demands, and other interests when you freelance full time. Give your writing the time and attention it deserves.

2. **Put everything you must do in a given day into a day planner, either printed or electronic.** This includes writing and all other tasks, both large and small. The more time you schedule for writing, the more successful you'll be.

3. **Think of writing as a business.** Hobbies rarely produce money. Most businesses do. The money you make is one of the big indicators distinguishing your business from a hobby.

4. **Do the things businesses do.** Get a separate checking account, business license, tax ID number, and business telephone listing. These are among the basics for getting your business started.

5. **Remind yourself to view your freelance writing as a business.** You'll be more apt to stick to your writing schedule and get more writing done when you do. That equals more money and more satisfaction for you.

6. **Have a writing space or office.** You need an area to call your own, whether it's a corner in the kitchen, an entire basement, or a bedroom of your home. You may have to think creatively to identify space that is not immediately obvious to you.

7. **Decorate your space.** Use items, colors, designs, and lighting that inspire you and put you in the writing mood. Writing is a more enjoyable experience when you feel welcome and comfortable in your space.

8. **Keep the space all to yourself.** Make your writing space completely off limits to your spouse, significant other, or kids. It's yours and yours alone. This is true even if your space is one part of one wall in the kitchen or the hallway.

9. **Develop a support network.** Writing can be a lonely experience if you let it be. Get out and mingle with others who support your goals rather than stay holed-up in your writing space every day around-the-clock.

10. **Vary your socializing.** Socializing is an important way to keep you and your writing fresh and alive. Meet a friend for coffee every Tuesday morning, or plan a date night once a week with your spouse or significant other.

11. **Interact frequently with people you know, like, and trust.** They can give you encouragement, ideas, and a breath of fresh air when you need it. You can return the favor when they need some support.

12. **Set boundaries with friends and family.** People are inclined to see you as "always being home" or "not really working" when you're a freelancer. They may drop by during the day to chat or insist you help them with daily errands. Tell them you have writing time and family or friends time. Tell them when those specific times are.

13. **Commit to regular work hours.** Choose any hours that work for you. Depending on your preferences, your office hours could be 9:00 AM to 5:00 PM Monday through Friday, or it can be 1 PM to 9 PM Wednesday through Sunday. Choose any hours and days that suit your creativity cycle. It's completely up to you as to your best work time and what other demands to consider in your life.

14. **Think like an entrepreneur, not an employee.** Entrepreneurs control their destiny. Employees let others take control of their future. Only you can control what happens in your writing business. Your clients can't, your spouse can't, and the economy can't. Taking charge of every situation is the only way you'll reap the rewards you desire.

15. **Visualize success.** Picture what you want your future to look like as specifically and frequently as possible. Include how much money you are earning, what kind of writing you are doing, where your writing space is located, and any other details you can. Your body and mind naturally work toward achieving the goal when you can clearly see your desired outcome.

Marketing Your Writing Business

16. **Join networking organizations.** One great way to generate business is to simply network. Attend business and community meetings, mingle with the crowd, and learn about the various writing services people are in need of.

17. **Secure your domain name.** Secure a domain name that matches your given name (www.dawnjosephson.com). If your name is already taken, then think of a domain name that tells what you do (www.dawnthewriter.com or www.masterwritingcoach.com).

18. **Create your website.** Tell the world what you do with a professional-looking website. Be mindful of your color choices and the overall feel of your site. Your content and design must convey professionalism at all times.

19. **Write a blog.** Your blog is a great way to showcase your writing talents. Blog about topics your ideal clients would find interesting. Give useful information that will prompt people to contact you.

20. **Create social media profiles.** Get your name known in the social media circles. By having a profile on Facebook, LinkedIn, Twitter, and Google+, and by posting useful updates and messages for your connections to see, you can keep your name circulating with your target clients.

21. **Listen to people when you attend networking functions.** They'll tell you exactly what they're looking for. This is more effective than dominating the conversation by bamboozling people with your skills and services.

22. **Develop a niche.** You simply can't write about every topic in existence, no matter how good a writer you are. That's why you need to define your niche or area(s) of expertise.

23. **Use word of mouth advertising to help grow your business.** By creating a niche, you can quickly become specialized and well-known in your chosen circle as a reliable writer who produces exceptional work. That word-of-mouth advertising is better than any ad you can place in any advertising outlet.

24. **Write for free to get publicity.** Locate trade publications that deal with your topics. Find these publications online by typing your category name into your favorite search engine. Look in books like *Writer's Market* for additional suggestions.

25. **Read the submission guidelines of trade publications.** Submit various articles that fit the publications' needs. Whether you make any money with these articles is not important at this point. Your immediate goal is to get some publicity.

26. **Write pieces for your local newspaper, community newsletter, or church weekly.** You never know what publications your potential clients read. You can usually get published very easily in these outlets. Now you'll have some

writing samples to show other publications and prospective clients.

27. **Run classified ads in writing and publishing association magazines and at writing web sites.** Write a short, 40-word classified ad that touts your writing services. Individuals and companies often go straight to writing related publications and sites when looking to hire freelance writers. Make it easy to find you.

28. **Team up with another company or freelancer, such as a graphic designer, to get more work.** Look for other companies or professionals who can benefit by offering their clients freelance writing services. For example, graphic designers are often great at laying out and designing written pieces. They're not usually skilled writers.

29. **Develop reciprocal deals with other professionals.** Both you and the person or company you're teaming up with must gain value from the relationship. You may choose to implement a formalized referral fee structure, or simply have a verbal understanding of mutual referrals without fees being exchanged. Be clear about the deal.

30. **Create a brand for yourself.** You must stand out from the thousands of other freelancers competing for the same assignments as you if you want to be a successful writer. Highlight that uniqueness, your brand, during all your conversations with potential clients and in your marketing materials.

31. **Follow up with potential leads.** So many freelance writers forget to follow up with potential clients. Your follow-up can be the single thing to distinguish you from among the rest.

32. **Call and email anyone who expresses an interest in your writing services.** Find out more about their needs. Listen carefully to what they say. Determine how you could best help. Offer solutions to their challenges and they'll be eager to hire you.

33. **Develop strong marketing materials.** Have a powerful information kit to give potential clients. Think about what to include and what to leave out. Both are important. Give this kit to anyone inquiring about your services, and be sure to follow up. Have physical copies on hand as well as the PDF version to email people.

34. **Choose your information kit contents carefully.** Provide samples of your best work, an overview of the writing services you provide, an indication of how you help people, your bio, your business card, and client testimonials.

35. **Be a shameless self-promoter.** You need to tell people about your writing services for them to know about you. Be willing to tout your services.

36. **Have information kits and business cards with you at all times**. Hand them out freely to anyone who expresses an interest. You never know who you'll run into or where one contact will lead you.

Day-to-Day Success

37. **Set your fees and stick with them.** Your rates will vary depending on your area of expertise, skill, and reputation within your niche circle. Many writers use the following formula to determine an approximate hourly rate when first starting out.

Required annual income + 30% (for expenses) + 30% (for benefits)
Divided by
Billable hours worked per year

Suppose you need to earn at least $40,000 per year:

$40,000 + $12,000 + $12,000
1,200 hours

Your total is $53.33 per hour. Round that total to either $50 or $55 per hour. Stick with that rate. You can gradually increase your fee as you gain experience.

38. **Set project rates.** For writing projects you do repeatedly, such as article writing or letter writing, set a flat project rate. You may opt for something like $500 per 1500-word article or $100 for a one-page letter. Clients like knowing a flat rate for a particular service.

39. **Use contracts in your work.** A contract in any profession is a legal document designed to protect both parties. A freelance writing contract is no different. Use a contract for every assignment or risk not getting paid and having no legal recourse to fall back on.

40. **Track your time accurately.** Have a reliable system for tracking your time when you bill by the hour. This avoids overcharging and under-billing your clients. Use one of the many time tracking apps available, such as Fanurio, Timely, or Timesheet, or choose a simple paper and pencil system. Write your start and stop time for every project with the handwritten system.

41. **Select the tracking method that works best for you.** The system you use depends on your preferences. Make sure whatever you choose is accurate. Be willing to change systems if you find one is not working well for you.

42. **Send invoices regularly.** You must invoice your clients if you want to be paid for your writing services. Send invoices either twice per month (on the 1st and 15th of each month), or every Friday for all work completed up to the invoice date.

43. **Indicate on your invoices that payment is due within 30 days or less.** You may decide to offer a discount for faster payment, or to generally make payment due in less than 30 days. People are unlikely to remember to pay you. Remind them with invoices.

44. **Accept credit cards.** Get a merchant account from your bank so you can accept credit cards as payment. You can also use PayPal for credit card payments. Investigate the best option for your situation.

45. **Delegate tasks that weigh you down.** Everyone has tasks they dislike or are not income-

producing. It might be filing, stuffing envelopes for marketing letters, or research. Determine which tasks you do regularly that get in your way of making serious money. Delegate those tasks to someone else.

46. **Be creative in your delegating**. Consider paying your own or a neighbor's kid to help you a few hours a week. Another option is an intern from a local college. Paying for this help buys you time and enthusiasm to devote to your core income producing activities.

47. **Delegate home tasks too.** If you didn't have to clean your house, mow your yard, or do your grocery shopping, how much more income-producing work could you do? Freeing up time by delegating home tasks to family or paid help can greatly increase your income (provided you use your newfound time to write).

48. **Hone your negotiation skills.** Be ready to negotiate with others to get paid what your writing services are truly worth. Take a seminar on negotiation skills, or read a book about the topic. Role-play negotiation scenarios with someone you trust. The better you're able to negotiate terms of an assignment, the more money you will make.

49. **Respond to voicemail messages promptly.** Return calls within 24 hours when a client or potential client leaves a message on your voicemail. Indicate on your outgoing message when you expect to return calls.

50. **Reply to e-mail as soon as possible.** People move on to someone else when they don't get the

information they need from you quickly. Someone else will get business that could have been yours.

51. **Pay your taxes.** Give Uncle Sam his fair share of your earnings, as unpleasant as that may be. Set aside about 30% of your income for taxes. That may be more than you need once you determine your allowable deductions.

52. **Set aside more money for taxes than necessary.** As you get a better idea of what your tax liability actually is, adjust the amount you set aside accordingly.

53. **Establish writing goals.** Determine how many written pieces you want to produce each week or month, and how much money you want to earn from each piece. Make your goals realistic and attainable.

54. **Post your goals where you'll see them every day.** Focus on your goals each day. They'll become reality before you know it.

55. **Stay confident and current in your skills.** You'll face rejection at some point in your writing business. This is a part of this business. Get over it and move on. Don't dwell on it or question your writing abilities.

56. **Learn what you need to know and then try again.** Sometimes a rejection is because you lack a certain skill. Consider adding that skill to what you know if it is an important addition to your services.

57. **Check your facts.** Verify the accuracy of a great quote or statistic to use in your piece. Go to the original source of information and confirm the data is still correct. Nothing ruins your writing reputation quicker than using outdated or inaccurate facts.

58. **Be faithful to your schedule.** If you say you're going to work on the Smith project for two hours, then do it for only two hours. Then move to your next scheduled item. All your projects deserve your best attention. Stick to the time you've allotted.

59. **Reschedule any items you bumped because of an emergency.** Things happen where you just can't stick to your schedule. Immediately reschedule what you changed so nothing gets lost along the way.

60. **Treat yourself as number one.** Plan time for yourself every day. You'll be better able to give your clients the quality work and service they deserve when you give yourself the respect and attention you deserve.

61. **Refuse work that compromises any of your values.** Look out for yourself and your own best interests. Stay true to yourself while helping clients and seeking as many writing assignments as possible.

62. **Give yourself a break.** Take breaks periodically as needed throughout the day. Plan one or more long or short vacations throughout the year. This is more a necessity than a luxury. Do whatever is possible to take these breaks.

63. **Recharge your creativity by giving your mind a break from writing.** You write better text in less time when you go back to your writing after that break.

64. **Expect highs and lows.** All business is cyclical. Some months are busy beyond belief, and others are so slow you'll wonder what to do with your time. This is simply the nature of having a business.

65. **Use your time well during business fluctuations.** Focus on your marketing efforts and plan your next business project during slow periods. The phone will start ringing again before you know it. You'll have more business than you can handle.

Working With Clients Effectively

66. **Stick to your word.** Do what you say you're going to do when you tell a client you're going to do something. Do it without excuses. Excuses weaken your credibility.

67. **Get in the habit of under-promising and over-delivering.** Doing anything less leads people to question your integrity and can quickly hurt your bottom line. This approach minimizes your own stress.

68. **Give honest estimates and quotes.** Nothing frustrates a client more than getting an estimate for four hours worth of work, and then getting billed for ten hours. Allow yourself time to think about your price for each job and to consider what is involved.

69. **Appear as the competent professional writer you are.** Get as much information about the job as possible. Quote your price based on that information rather than out of desperation and best-guess just to get the project.

70. **Develop your people skills as well as your writing skills.** Running a successful writing business is as much about networking and interacting with people as it is about actual writing.

71. **Practice your people skills regularly.** Do this so you can quickly build rapport with others even if you're a natural introvert. People give you their business when they feel comfortable with you.

72. **Care about your clients.** Your clients are people and have everyday challenges, just like you. Get to know them a little deeper and find out about their life. Learn when their birthday is. Find out if they have kids in school. Ask what got them involved in their current career.

73. **Make small talk with your clients when appropriate.** Inquire about how their family is doing. Show an interest in their business. People like to feel cared about. They'll be more interested in working with you again and again when you show a genuine interest in them.

74. **Give your clients multiple touches.** Communicate with past clients. Use those relationships rather than constantly looking for new work. It's easier, less expensive, and more rewarding to do it this way.

75. **Create a system for contacting your past clients.** Send them mailings and emails regularly to remind them of your services. Call them once a month to see how you can help them. Send them articles of interest you find online or in magazines.

76. **Show appreciation.** Tell your clients "thank you" on a regular basis. Let them know you value your relationship with them and that you enjoy working with them. Do this by a phone call, a personal handwritten note, or even a small gift when appropriate.

77. **Be friendly, but not too friendly, with clients.** The more you work with certain clients, the more you'll develop a close relationship with them. That's okay as long as you keep the relationship

professional at all times. You could compromise the professionalism of the relationship by getting too friendly with clients. This might lead to hurt feelings down the road.

78. **Be open to new viewpoints.** Your clients will likely have various views on topics. Their viewpoints may be different from yours. You must be able to accept, not necessarily agree with, different viewpoints to work effectively with your clients.

79. **View it as a learning experience when someone thinks differently from you.** This is far superior to getting defensive or trying to convert them to your thinking. Find out all you can about the new perspective. You may learn something that changes your mind.

80. **Ask for money when you deserve it.** Speak up when a client is slow in paying you. Send a simple reminder in the mail, or call to find out if they already mailed a payment. Most people are honest and want to pay you. They simply get caught up in the demands of life and forget. Your reminder helps them get back on track.

81. **Tell the truth, even when it hurts.** Say so when you can't take on a project because you don't have the expertise or the time to do it. Tell a client you think their idea is a flop if that's what you believe. Telling the truth can sometimes hurt, but it rewards you in the long-run.

82. **Offer an alternative idea to the client.** If a client has a bad idea, present a suggestion to modify the client's idea so that it will work. Refer a client to

someone else when you know you can't help the client.

83. **Keep all information confidential.** You will naturally learn things the general population does not know when doing writing assignments for people. Ask your client if it's okay for you share your new knowledge before you blurt it out to others. You don't want to give away trade secrets or proprietary information. When in doubt, keep confidential what others tell you.

84. **Know when to cut ties.** Sometimes you'll encounter a client who is difficult to work with, who drains you emotionally, or who wastes more time than they pay for. Have the courage to let the client go when you feel they are not your ideal client or are not profitable to work with. Refer them to someone who may be better qualified to help.

Sustained Business and Personal Growth

85. **Invest in good equipment.** Having the right technology is key as a writer. Install the computer word processing programs for your needs. Use a fast and clean printer with no smudges. Use a reliable Internet connection. You'll do most of your business online. Your equipment must be up to par.

86. **Put money in the bank.** Put at least 10% of everything you earn into a savings account for your business. Divide that big check you got from a client today. Spend some and save some.

87. **Have at least two months worth of business income saved at all times.** That saved money helps stay afloat if your writing business runs into a slump. Some people advise a six-month cushion to ease your overall concerns. Save an amount that makes sense for you and your situation.

88. **Create a basic budget.** Businesses need budgets to stay profitable. Include categories for marketing materials, advertisements, professional association dues, utilities, taxes, postage, technology, savings, and what you plan to pay yourself. Consider these the basics to be in business.

89. **Look where your business money goes each month.** Create additional categories accordingly. Determine how much you spend in each category. Stick to those numbers as much as possible. The more closely you follow your budget, the more money you'll have left in your pocket.

90. **Keep a strong sense of humor.** Goof-ups and mishaps happen. Find humor in everything instead of focusing on negatives in the situation. The way the sentence reads with that typo probably really *is* funny. Put yourself at ease and make learning from your mistakes easier by laughing at yourself and your mistakes.

91. **Be flexible.** Sometimes due dates change, or the scope of your writing project alters due to some newly uncovered information. This is normal and part of the writing life.

92. **Be willing to accept changes.** Do your best to keep the project on schedule. The more flexibility you can have, the more success you'll experience.

93. **Stay committed.** Running a successful writing business takes perseverance, no matter how much you enjoy it. Your determination and vision pull you through any business slump.

94. **Keep your goals firmly in mind**. Let them guide you through any slow periods or times of doubt. Reflect on your goals daily. Commit to making your freelance career work no matter what.

95. **Expand your offerings.** Offer additional services or products that make sense. For example, could you coach people to be better writers? Offer books or reports on topics of interest to your clients? Oversee clients' social media or blog posts? Think creatively about other services, products, or information your clients might need and see how you can fulfill that need.

96. **Take educated risks.** Businesses grow when the owner takes a few risks. The same applies to your freelance writing business. Analyze the pros and cons if you want to expand into a new writing topic, for instance. Make your move if it looks promising.

97. **Realize that no risk is 100% fail proof.** Know both the rewards and consequences of a decision to increase the likelihood of a positive outcome. Your risks can pay off handsomely when well considered.

98. **Know when it's time to secure outside office space.** You may outgrow your home-based writing space when you need to hire additional help, have too many projects for your space, or need more privacy than your current home office space provides. These are all valid reasons for feeling the need to look elsewhere.

99. **Search for convenient, safe, and fairly-priced space.** Rent for a small office is fairly inexpensive compared to the income your increased productivity brings. Decorate the outside office space based on the colors, lighting, and other details you found important for your space at home.

100. **Do an annual review of what worked and what didn't.** Review the milestones your business made, as well as the flops you encountered at the end of each year. Identify what you can repeat from the successes and what you can do differently from the failures.

101. **Compare your goals to your annual year end review.** You may find a need to modify some goals, or that you have new insights leading you to a goal sooner.

ABOUT THE AUTHOR

Dawn Josephson empowers leaders to master the printed word for enhanced credibility, positioning, and profits. As an editor and ghostwriter, she helps her clients create irresistible books, articles, and blog posts that position them as the expert. And in her work as a freelance writing business consultant, she helps new and established freelance writers achieve and exceed their career objectives.

Dawn got her first piece published at age 8. Today she has over 5,000 published articles and 30 published books to add to her list of accomplishments, many of which are published under her clients' names. Her client list includes professional speakers, business owners, attorneys, accountants, physicians, book and magazine publishers, infomercial celebrities, business consultants and coaches, psychologists, real estate professionals, Olympic athletes, college professors, and even an astronaut.

Dawn is a recognized expert in her field and is known for her straightforward writing, humor, and bold approach. She has been featured in such media outlets as *Huffington Post, USA Today, Investor's Business Daily, PR News, HR Magazine, Job Placement & Training Report, Educational Dealer, Real Estate Broker's Insider, Writer's Weekly,* and other national publications.

Dawn is the author of two internationally acclaimed books, *Putting It On Paper: The Ground Rules for Creating Promotional Pieces that Sell Books* and *Write It Right: The Ground Rules for Self-Editing Like the Pros.*

www.ingramcontent.com/pod-product-compliance
Lightning Source LLC
Chambersburg PA
CBHW060500200326
41520CB00017B/4866